EACH DAY DIES WITH SLEEP

José Rivera

BROADWAY PLAY PUBLISHING INC
New York
www.broadwayplaypublishing.com
info@broadwayplaypublishing.com

EACH DAY DIES WITH SLEEP
© Copyright 1990 by José Rivera

All rights reserved. This work is fully protected under the copyright laws of the United States of America. No part of this publication may be photocopied, reproduced, stored in a retrieval system, or transmitted, in any form or by any means, electronic, mechanical, recording, or otherwise, without the prior permission of the publisher. Additional copies of this play are available from the publisher.

Written permission is required for live performance of any sort. This includes readings, cuttings, scenes, and excerpts. For amateur and stock performances, please contact Broadway Play Publishing Inc. For all other rights also please contact the author c/o B P P I.

First acting edition printing: November 2004
Second printing: September 2014

I S B N: 978-0-88145-246-4

Book design: Marie Donovan
Typeface: Palatino
Printed and bound in the U S A

ORIGINAL PRODUCTION

EACH DAY DIES WITH SLEEP received its world premiere on 10 April 1990 in a co-production by Circle Repertory Theater (Tanya Berezin, Artistic Director) and Berkeley Repertory Theater (Sharon Ott, Artistic Director).

NELLY	Erica Gimpel
AUGIE	Alex Colón
JOHNNY	Randy Vasquez
Director	Roberta Levitow
Set design	Tom Kamm
Costume design	Tina Cantu Navarro
Lighting design	Robert Wierzel
Sound design (Berkeley)	Barney Jones
Sound design (New York)	Janet Kalas
Scenic projection design	Charles Rose
Prop design	Skip Epperson
Original music	Rebeca Mauleon & Joe Taylor
Dramaturg (Berkeley)	Mame Hunt
Dramaturg (New York)	Adrienne Heigel
Stage manager (Berkeley)	Meryl Lind Shaw
Stage manager (New York)	Fred Reinglas

The premiere of the play was made possible, in part, with a grant from the Rockefeller Foundtion and with public funds from the National Endowment for the Arts, the New York State Council on the Arts and the New York City Department of Cultural Affairs. The premiere was also a part of the "A T & T New Plays for the Nineties Project".

CHARACTERS & SETTING

NELLY, *a woman in ther twenties*
AUGIE, *her father, in his forties*
JOHNNY, *her husband, in his thirties*

Place: NELLY's *home on the East Coast and* NELLY's *home in Los Angeles*

Time: The present. The play covers several years.

ACT ONE

1

(Three playing areas: a furnished room center, flanked by two small empty areas. There's a door in the center area and one in the small area L. There's an engine block in the area R. All areas are dark.)

(Lively guitar music is heard. An image of an orange tree is projected on a wall.)

(Lights up center. There are strangely shaped windows, a dusty, beat-up old couch and worn, overstuffed chairs in this room. Everything looks a hundred years old.)

(NELLY, early twenties, is sitting on the floor in the center room, surrounded by a mountain of freshly cleaned socks. There are hundreds of socks. NELLY is trying to find matching pairs. She's in desperate need of sleep.)

(By her side is a toy truck which she periodically plays with like a spastic child.)

(Feeling hungry, NELLY goes to the sofa. She's hidden some food under the cushions. She finds her food and eats fast.)

(She notices the image of the orange tree. She giggles. She claps her hands and the image changes: we see the Pacific Ocean. This makes her so happy, she laughs.)

(A gunshot is heard offstage. The images disappear.)

(NELLY's father, AUGIE, enters, dodging the shot we just heard. AUGIE is a robust Latino in his late forties.)

(JOHNNY *appears, playing the guitar. He's a handsome, beautifully-built man, early thirties. He watches this scene, unnoticed.*)

AUGIE: *(Whispers to* NELLY*)* What's wrong with those animals? Why are they shooting at their own father? *(Shouting to ceiling)* You kids better get to bed! Stop shooting off guns or I'll come up there with my belt!

(Guitar music stops. We hear hundreds of footsteps as an army of children run to their bedrooms. Dozens of doors are slammed.)

(Silence. AUGIE *smiles triumphantly.* NELLY's *too afraid to look at him.)*

(Note: in the first two scenes, NELLY *has trouble speaking, as if her mouth were unable to keep up with her rapid mind. Her vocal rhythm, volume or speed are always off. It's a struggle.)*

NELLY: It's three o'clock! In the morning! What'd you expect—a hero's welcome?

AUGIE: ...And lucky me gets to come home to the pinhead. *(He staggers toward the offstage bedroom. He opens the door, starts to exit, but is repulsed by an incredible smell coming from the room.)* How can I sleep in there? Your mother smells like a forest of dead animals. Is it any wonder I go PARTYING?

(He reenters the center room. Frightened, NELLY *springs to her feet and runs around on all fours. Walking on all fours is the only way she can get around.)*

NELLY: Do not come near me! Go away!

AUGIE: And what're the little assassins doing up? On a school night? Huh, Pinhead?

NELLY: I am not Pinhead! Say my *real* name, Dad—

AUGIE: Not *homework*, right? My offshoots aren't up there doing their *homework*. They're up there *plotting*.

ACT ONE 3

Making secret plans to waste me. Well it's not going to work. I'm too smart.

(AUGIE *pours himself a drink.* NELLY *glares at him.*)

NELLY: *(Sarcastic)* Have a drink.

AUGIE: Don't sass me, Pinhead.

(*Before he drinks,* AUGIE *takes out a deck of tarot cards. He flips them over, studying them carefully, looking for omens.*)

(NELLY *looks at* AUGIE *angrily and holds out her hand.*)

NELLY: Hey! *So where's my birthday present?*

AUGIE: *(Flipping cards)* Sorry, Pinhead, I decided tonight: *no more celebrating birthdays.* I can't remember twenty-one birthdays. And your mother won't get her heaving bulk out of bed to help me. So from now on, we celebrate *one* birthday, *my* birthday, a day we can all rejoice in, like the birth of Jesus.

(*Disappointed,* NELLY *plays with the truck to keep from crying*)

AUGIE: Taste this for me. The cards look ominous.

(NELLY *tastes the drink. She's gripped by convulsions. She trembles horribly and falls over head.* AUGIE *doesn't blink.*)

AUGIE: One passionate night, I swear, I'm gonna launch a preemptive strike and erase *all* you kids from the world. Then I'll start over *fresh*, with a sexy young wife, and twenty-one new children *who will love me.*

(NELLY *dog-walks offstage.*)

NELLY: *(Off)* Maybe this time? You'll remember their names?

(AUGIE *starts undressing for bed. He strips down to his shorts.*)

AUGIE: I can still make babies, you know. Don't question that. I can get *trees* pregnant. I'm a one-man human reforestation program.

(NELLY *comes back on with a bucket of warm water. She sniffs* AUGIE's *fingers.*)

NELLY: Your fingers smell like *two* women. Girls! Young! Stupid!

AUGIE: *(Laughs)* Yeah, they were very young all right. And very stupid.

NELLY: Oh go clean up! I smell adultery in your pores and I'm gagging!

AUGIE: Aw, leave me alone, my day sucked. It all started this morning with the sound of Raphael's screams as Sylvia whaled on his face with a crescent wrench. Then it was Hector's screams 'cause he's drowning in the blood of Raphael's massive nosebleed and would have died if I hadn't performed mouth-to-mouth C P R on him. Then the assassination attempts started. Floating like an oil slick in my coffee was Liquid Draino. I was in the tub? And one of your doomed siblings dropped a live radio in the water. Sizzled the hair off my legs! All that before breakfast! At lunch, Rosaline sets Anita's cat on fire and the cat's running around the house, its organs bubbling and eyes sizzling, and Roberto's brought home by the cops in handcuffs for extorting money in school from the first graders, and Marcus Junior's got an olive pit so far up his nose it's playing pinball with his goddamn brains! And this social worker's got the brass balls to say the way out of my poverty is sterilization— "I will not be sterilized!" —I said, as I threw her through a window on the second floor.

(NELLY *dries* AUGIE's *feet. Contented,* AUGIE *lies on the couch, his bed for the night.* NELLY *jumps on his stomach like a heavy cat.* AUGIE *groans.*)

ACT ONE 5

NELLY: My name? My name? Remember my name?

AUGIE: Why're you always *at* me about your goddamn name? I draw a blank on your name.

NELLY: Notice? You have twenty-one children. I'm the *only* one staying up late, making sure you're not homecoming stabbed in the heart. Only me! I care!

AUGIE: Yeah. Why is that? You want something? An allowance?

NELLY: Yes! To hear my *name*!

AUGIE: I forgot it.

NELLY: It's Nelly...*Nelly*...you sad big fool!

(NELLY *jumps off* AUGIE *and sits on the floor. She plays with the truck and cries quietly.*)

AUGIE: Awwwwwwww. Are you pouting? Don't get enough love?

NELLY: *(Pointing to herself)* I'm a slave. Workhorse. Sock cleaner. Cook. And I am not sleeping well! Not slept since the last full moon: I'm the janitor for twenty brothers and sisters.

AUGIE: *(Laughing)* Hey. Can't blame me for all those kids. I haven't touched your mother in years. The sun gets her pregnant. Cockroaches and clouds get her pregnant: the *horny moon*. That's why your brothers and sisters are so friggin' weird. And I swear her pregnancies are getting shorter and shorter all the time!

(NELLY *tries to stand up. It takes great effort and she almost succeeds.* AUGIE *watches her struggle, frightened. Her speech is almost "normal."*)

NELLY: Don't turn around too fast, Dad—don't blink too hard—or you'll see me gone.

AUGIE: *(Alarmed)* Are you going to leave me, Pinhead?

NELLY: I daydreamed about California! California sun!

AUGIE: Quit saying that! I'm your father! Show some respect!

NELLY: You're not my father 'til you remember my name! Drunk old pig!

(AUGIE *lunges at* NELLY. *She screams and runs on all fours, throwing socks at him.* AUGIE *is too drunk and tired to chase her. He fixes another drink.*)

(*There's a loud groaning noise offstage, like wood scraping against wood.*)

AUGIE: *(Frightened by the noise)* What's that? That the house? Is it my imagination or is this house getting *bigger*? I'm walking up the driveway tonight, looking up and up and up...and there are new *windows* up there.

NELLY: The house is an organism. Reproducing like you do. Like children and rooms are unimportant and don't need to be cared for.

(AUGIE *laughs, scared.*)

AUGIE: If I care for one of you, I have to care for all of you, and who's got that much time?

NELLY: *(On the attack)* The house is like you. Full of lies. Sick dreams. I don't know the real number of rooms: there's the television room, the sex room, the room of endless hunger, the room of storms, the room of teardrops, the rooms of moss and mushrooms. There are animals all over the house! They're just cubs now. Just baby carnivores. But they will grow. I don't want to be around then! No thanks cleaning animal shit all my life!

(AUGIE *looks at her.*)

AUGIE: It's Alicia! Your name is Alicia!

ACT ONE

(JOHNNY *strums the guitar.* AUGIE *grabs* NELLY *around the waist, makes her stand upright and dances with her as* JOHNNY *plays.* NELLY *tries to squirm free, but can't.*)

AUGIE: Sleep with me.

NELLY: *(Shocked)* I'm your daughter.

AUGIE: I don't know that. There are so many people living here who I don't know, you could be the new social worker or something....

(AUGIE *laughs drunkenly and continues dancing as* NELLY *continues to squirm.* AUGIE *smiles at a recent memory.*)

AUGIE: I was on the dance floor tonight. A girl's tongue was in my ear, tickling the lose nerves in my brain. She scrambled my memories until I didn't know who I was anymore. It was great.

(*A woman screams, offstage.* AUGIE *and* NELLY *look at each other.*)

NELLY: There's no avoiding her. The mammoth woman. She can smell your nasty fingertips.

(AUGIE *falls asleep in* NELLY's *arms.* JOHNNY *continues playing.* AUGIE *dances as* NELLY *pulls him toward the area L. She opens the door and pushes him into the offstage bedroom. She closes the door.*)

(*Exhausted,* NELLY *goes to the center room, tries to sleep on the sofa, but can't. We see projections of dreamlike black and white clouds. Lights suggest the passage of time.*)

2

(*As* NELLY *tosses and turns,* JOHNNY *gets down on his belly and crawls across the floor, commando-style, toward the area R. The face of a pretty young woman, with the word "Gloria" over it, is projected.* NELLY *sees* JOHNNY *and jumps on his back, squashing him. She laughs.*)

NELLY: You've got teflon balls, little horsie! Big metal balls!

JOHNNY: Get off my back, Nelly!

NELLY: Where're you going? Upstairs? At five o'clock in the morning, Johnny??

JOHNNY: Felicia's room—

NELLY: *Felicia's!?* You dumped Lizbeth so soon?! *(Hitting him)* Slime! Disease! Pestilence! *(Goes to* AUGIE's *door and pounds on it)* Hey Dad! Wake up!

(JOHNNY *grabs* NELLY *and pulls her away from the door. They struggle violently*

JOHNNY: Hey! I don't want that son-of-a-bitch to see me!

(JOHNNY *pins her down. He's on top of her. They look at each other.* JOHNNY *tries to kiss her. She pushes his mouth away.)*

NELLY: Yuck! Your spit tastes like gasoline!

(She bites him on the arm. He yowls and jumps off her, rubbing his arm in pain.)

JOHNNY: So? Okay, I love you. Those weird-color eyes of yours make me nuts. Admit you love me too.

NELLY: Admit all your bastards. Felicia's three kids! Maritza's twins! Nilda's retarded son! Yours!

JOHNNY: Will you slow *down*? You think too fast for your mouth—

NELLY: My nieces and nephews are all your babies—

JOHNNY: Oh man. That's beat. That's just a rumor.

NELLY: The bastards play guitar. Flex muscles. Comb hair. Like you do.

JOHNNY: *(Combing hair)* Coincidence.

(He smiles at her. She scampers away. He follows.)

ACT ONE

JOHNNY: Awwww, just admit you love me, Nelly, c'mon.

NELLY: Oh. Go to Felicia. I don't care.

JOHNNY: I can skip Felicia. I always thought you were prettier. I just thought you were too young and weird—

NELLY: It's my birthday tonight! I got no presents!

JOHNNY: I'm your present. I know you look at me. A guy can tell. You're not the pinhead everyone says.

NELLY: I am not stupid!

JOHNNY: And you get me riled up the way you crawl around on all fours and misuse your pronouns. Do you think I'm good-looking? Do you?

NELLY: *(Soft)* Maybe. Confused. Don't trust you.

(JOHNNY *comes toward* NELLY *again, but she runs away, pointing at the projection.*)

NELLY: *No!* You love Gloria.

JOHNNY: Gloria? No! She's a, she's a *girl*. Sixteen. A stick.

NELLY: You're killing time—waiting for puberty to explode her—then you'll pounce her bones and forget me.

JOHNNY: I've been waiting for *you*! To walk and talk right. I see improvement. I know just being with me is making you better all the time. *(Tries to touch her)* Nelly, Nelly, I play guitar like the wind.

(NELLY *stands completely straight for the first time in the play. It's a struggle. He looks at her extremely surprised.*)

NELLY: You hurt Maritza, then Nilda, then Lizbeth, then Felicia. That's a disgusting track record!

JOHNNY: But don't you think I'm beautiful?

(She's back on all fours. She plays with the truck, ignoring him, which he can't stand.)

JOHNNY: You're right. I made it with all your big sisters. I knocked them all up. What can I say? I love this family.

(NELLY turns away disgusted.)

JOHNNY: I can't help what nature's done to me. It's some magic I got. I'm a victim. I'm too beautiful to live.

(JOHNNY grabs her, holding her still.)

JOHNNY: You make me feel different than your sisters do. I never met a woman who could resist me. How can you do that? How come you're the only one? You know how crazy that makes me get?

(He tries to kiss her; she pulls away, still standing.)

NELLY: I will not be your next casualty, Johnny Amengual.

JOHNNY: Boy, your syntax has really picked up.

NELLY: If Nelly and Johnny...*exist*...the buck stops here. We stay together. There's no Gloria after me. I am forever or nothing.

JOHNNY: That's a long time.

NELLY: Not worth it? Think about this.

(NELLY kisses him viciously. Then she pushes him away roughly. The kiss stuns JOHNNY.)

NELLY: That's so—you know what—you give up—if you hurt me. *(She kisses him again. She is tender. She pushes him away tenderly.)* That's. A memory of me. Burned in your skin. Your nerves will haunt you with that memory, drive you to a crazy suicide—and blast you—to a million, lovesick stars.

(NELLY crawls to the socks. JOHNNY is reeling from her kiss.)

ACT ONE

JOHNNY: What'd you do to my mouth? WHAT WAS THAT? That wasn't human, Nelly.

NELLY: Magic? Me?

JOHNNY: I've never—in my whole life—tasted—who knew you could do that?!

NELLY: *(Dismissing him)* Felicia? Waiting?

JOHNNY: How can I kiss Felicia after this? You ruined me!

NELLY: *(Pointing to projection)* Gloria? Bitch?

JOHNNY: Gloria who? Nelly, let's get married, tonight, please, we gotta.

(NELLY *laughs.*)

JOHNNY: Hey, this isn't easy for me, so don't laugh! But the truth is, I'm getting too old for this. Breaking into your father's castle, slithering up endless flights of stairs, through gloomy bedrooms and weird animals. I need you to help me grow up, like I'm helping you talk.

(JOHNNY *kisses* NELLY. *She continues working on the socks, unfazed.*)

JOHNNY: C'mon, what do you want from me?

NELLY: Employment history. I want to know your prospects.

JOHNNY: My what?

NELLY: Johnny. I'm the—middle—child of twenty-one children—number eleven. *I haven't left this house in two years.* No more! I have to know what I'm getting into with you. Want prospects. Want better.

JOHNNY: I have prospects. I'm going to quit working on cars and make money on my knockout looks. Be a fashion model.

NELLY: No prospects.

(She angrily grabs him by the lapels and shakes him.)

NELLY: I have ideas! Bursting my skull to *make* something. I don't want to watch and worry over brothers and sisters the rest of a—short—life.

JOHNNY: Like what ideas?

NELLY: My plan is this: I can fall asleep and dream winning lottery numbers. I can win big bucks real fast.

JOHNNY: You can?

NELLY: Make big bucks. Move to California. Away from Dad. Open a garage. Fix Porsches, Mercedes, Jaguars. You and me. We'll be a team and we'll be rich, Johnny.

JOHNNY: But fixing cars is so *boring*....

NELLY: *Want* boring. There's too much excitement in my life. I don't want any more violence, hunger, and screaming babies. I want to sleep eight hours a day. Every day of the week. Johnny. *(Touches his face tenderly)* You're thirty-five years old. You're still living with your Mami. You don't have the drive. I have the drive. *I want to go.* Go together?

JOHNNY: Are you using me?

*(*NELLY *enthusiastically nods yes.)*

JOHNNY: Oh. But you can walk out of here without me. You don't need me.

NELLY: *I do!* Do you notice? My brothers and sisters never leave the house. Why? My father's tyrant-blood is in us. His blood controls us. Keeps us afraid.

JOHNNY: I'm not afraid of him.

NELLY: I know! Your hate for him is in my blood now. It's going to help me escape him.

ACT ONE

(NELLY *kisses* JOHNNY. *The projection of Gloria disappears.* NELLY *smiles.*)

NELLY: Want you. Marry you.

JOHNNY: No. "I want to marry you." Say it.

NELLY: "I want to marry you."

JOHNNY: I want to marry you too. I want to have sex with you first.

NELLY: Can't sex here. I have no bedroom here.

(*We see projections of children sleeping two and three to a bed.*)

NELLY: Every night, I wander. From room to room. Looking for pieces of the floor not covered by members of my big family or animal droppings. But even in this house, with its hundred rooms, I share space with somebody. If I *do* fall asleep, I can't rest. My different-color eyes are always in conflict and they keep me awake. (*Stands up and walks normally, though with some effort. Her speech is nearly flawless.*) The blue eye hates the gray eye for something the gray eye did to the blue eye when I was still a fetus floating like a little fish in my mother's huge body. Floating there among the schools of unborn brothers and sisters. Today, the fighting between my eyes gives me headaches, Johnny, and prophetic dreams. (*Smiles at him*) Help me rest. I'll stop using you. I'll love you—fiercely—for the rest of my life.

JOHNNY: I think you're beautiful. Do you think I'm beautiful?

NELLY: Right now? I think you're very, very....

(NELLY *falls asleep.* JOHNNY *lifts her and starts to carry her offstage. As he approaches the exit, the projection of Gloria comes back on.* JOHNNY *stops to look at the beautiful Gloria.*)

3

(It's morning. AUGIE *enters the center room wearing party clothes.* JOHNNY *sees* AUGIE *and quickly puts* NELLY *down. She sleeps standing up. Frightened,* JOHNNY *crawls out of the house.)*

*(*NELLY *is seized by violent dreams as the projections of the black and white clouds return. She twists and shakes as the following are also rapidly projected:* AUGIE *in a wheelchair,* JOHNNY *wearing a white mask, a severed hand, a burning car, a burning house.)*

*(*AUGIE—*hung over, brittle—goes to* NELLY *and shakes her. She wakes up. The projections disappear. From this point on,* NELLY *walks and speaks normally. She looks at* AUGIE *a moment, getting her courage up.)*

NELLY: I'm going to California with Johnny Amengual. And you can't stop me.

*(*NELLY *starts throwing the socks offstage and into the audience. She dances happily around the stage, a free woman. The orange tree is projected on the wall.)*

AUGIE: What are you doing upright?

NELLY: Blame Johnny.

AUGIE: And speaking sequentially? Is this a joke?

NELLY: I'm a fast learner.

AUGIE: Then learn me some breakfast and clean socks, Pinhead. I have a party to go to. I need to be fresh.

NELLY: No more socks! I have found life outside of socks and hard labor!

AUGIE: I don't like this new turn of events here.

ACT ONE

NELLY: From now on my life will be filled with transmissions, batteries, windshields, flat tires, and money, money, money.

(NELLY *starts to leave.* AUGIE *claps his hands and* NELLY *freezes in her tracks.*)

AUGIE: You going to California? With Johnny Amengual? Felicia's boyfriend?

NELLY: My fiancé

AUGIE: Why? A man finally looks at you and you think it's love?

NELLY: He's kind.

AUGIE: Do you know how many of your nieces and nephews are his children?

NELLY: He hates you. He gives me strength.

AUGIE: No man should be that pretty. I hate that face of his. It drives me crazy those perfect bones, those dog eyes—

NELLY: I'm going—

AUGIE: *(Laughs)* And I thought you were the smart one of the family!

NELLY: Liar. You never thought of me as anything. I never crossed that sick cesspool frontier you call a *mind*, Dad. Let me stay anonymous. Let Lizbeth and Maritza take care of you, I'm out. *(She tries to leave.)*

AUGIE: Another step. And I'll smack your face across the goddamn room. *(Takes off his belt)* Then I'll get rough.

(NELLY *stops. She knows the threat is real.*)

NELLY: I'm not just me. I'm two people.

AUGIE: The pinhead can walk and talk and think. Well, golly. *(Laughs. Puts belt on)* I couldn't stop your idiot sisters from falling for Johnny Amengual. Guess I can't stop you.

NELLY: *(A chant)* I am Johnny. Johnny is me. I am Johnny—

AUGIE: But if you're going to get married, you're going to follow family *tradition*. You and Johnny will move in, take the top floor, and raise your big family in my house.

NELLY: Why do you want to do that to me?

AUGIE: You don't love Johnny.

NELLY: You don't know me.

AUGIE: I can see it in your eye. Your left eye. The gray one. The one I gave you. It's saying: you're only using him and you know he's going to run to Gloria the day she turns legal.

NELLY: I don't think so. I don't think I'm so easy to read anymore.

(NELLY *starts to go again.* AUGIE *grabs her, suddenly very afraid.)*

AUGIE: If you go, who's going to taste my coffee and make sure there's no Draino in it? Huh?!

NELLY: Dad—

AUGIE: And you can't leave me alone with your mother. She's a cannibal. She's been trying to swallow me. You know her appetite. I'm going with you to California.

NELLY: I'm going out that door to run across the street to Johnny's car. Try and follow me, Dad.

AUGIE: I'll be right behind you.

NELLY: Do it. You're not going to make it to the other side. I saw it in a dream. You're going to get hit by a car.

AUGIE: Liar.

NELLY: Look in my left eye and tell me I'm lying.

(AUGIE *looks in her eye. We and* AUGIE *see the projection of* AUGIE *in the wheelchair, a broken man.*)

AUGIE: That's—that's—

NELLY: *(Quickly kisses him)* Goodbye. *(She runs off.)*

AUGIE: That's—that's a *lie*!

(AUGIE *runs after her. We see a projection of a car coming down a busy street.*)

NELLY: *(Offstage)* Follow me! Follow me, Dad! Follow meeeeeeeeee!

(We hear AUGIE *scream and see a projection of a closeup of* AUGIE's *contorted face. A trickle of blood forms where* AUGIE's *mouth is, and runs down, bright red, the length of the projection screen.)*

4

(The projection of AUGIE *fades out.* NELLY *enters. She sadly wipes the blood from the screen with a sponge. She exits. Lights down on all the rooms.)*

5

(Lights up on area L. NELLY *enters, pushing* AUGIE *in a wheelchair.* AUGIE *is paralyzed from the waist down. He wears battered pajamas. On his lap is a small radio, a yoyo, a telephone, a shaving basin, razor, and shaving cream. His eyes, though still bright, are now full of fear and confusion.)*

(A spotlight reveals JOHNNY, *in the area R, now a garage.* JOHNNY *is dressed as a mechanic, working on the car engine.)*

(The center room remains dark.)

(We hear dozens of feet running around. Then dozens of cars being started. They all drive away until there's silence.)

(NELLY shaves AUGIE.)

NELLY: I talked to Mom. She, uh, didn't want you sleeping in the same bed as her. She says looking at you gets her depressed. *(Beat)* And I can't stay anymore.

(AUGIE violently shakes his head back and forth.)

NELLY: Dad! Johnny's in Los Angeles waiting for me. He opened a garage and bought a pretty little house on Laurel Canyon Blvd. with our lottery money.

(In the center room, in the dark, JOHNNY puts up an orange tree. During the following JOHNNY also fills the center room with new furniture.)

NELLY: He says "Nelly and Johnny's" is doing great. Hired two men to work under him. And he never talks about modeling. He's growing up. Says he misses me.

(AUGIE starts to cry.)

NELLY: It's going to be fine here. Mom's going to be a different woman. She's going to get out of bed and exercise. Do toe touches and leg lifts. And she says she's going to spend every penny of the insurance money on your comfort. Blow your nose.

(NELLY holds a handkerchief for AUGIE. He blows his nose.)

NELLY: You have to trust her. There's no one else. The kids and grandkids have left. The spell you had on their blood is broken. They've dispersed all over the world and left no forwarding addresses.

(AUGIE starts to cry.)

NELLY: Dad! This is no time to get sentimental about children you never gave a shit about. Stop it or I leave.

ACT ONE

(AUGIE *stops crying.*)

NELLY: One more thing. Your children left their pets behind. There are bears and monkeys and snakes and wild dogs living in the house. They're a little hungry. But don't worry. Mom's going to keep this door locked. *(Plugs the telephone into the wall)* I have a lot to do in California. I have to make up for all those years gibbering like an idiot and running around like a dog. I've got a five year-plan. *(Demonstrates the yoyo)* See? Isn't this fun?

(JOHNNY *looks at her across the distance of three thousand miles.*)

JOHNNY: Forget him. We have things to do, babe.

NELLY: I have to go.

(JOHNNY *exits.* NELLY *kisses* AUGIE *and exits.* AUGIE's *wife's laughter is heard offstage. The laughter reaches a peak*—AUGIE *covers his ears—then stops. Lights down on* AUGIE.)

6

(*Lights up on center room, now* NELLY *and* JOHNNY's *living room in Los Angeles. Lots of sunshine streams in through the windows. Growing out of the floor is the orange tree, heavy with ripe oranges. The roots of the tree extend the length and breadth of the room.* JOHNNY *runs on, chased by* NELLY, *who is shaking up a bottle of champagne. She sprays champagne all over* JOHNNY.)

NELLY: To our one-thousandth repair! Wooooooooooooo-ooooooo-eeeeee!

JOHNNY: Whooooooooo-oooooooooooo-eeeeeeeeee!!

NELLY: *(Drinking)* Whooooooooo-eeeeeeeeeee-he-he-he-he!!

(NELLY *hands* JOHNNY *the bottle of champagne and he drinks from it.*)

JOHNNY: Have you had one of these oranges? They're insane. (*Picks an orange from the tree, slices it in half and eats it*) Hhmmmmmmmmmm. They're *intoxicating.*

(NELLY *eats an orange. She reacts as if electricity has shot through her.*)

NELLY: Hmmmmmmmmmmmmmmmm. They make you dizzy!

JOHNNY: Hmmmmmmmmmmmmmmmmmmm.

NELLY: (*Intoxicated*) California is clean. And bright. And modern. And sleek. And do you think everyone in Los Angeles has an orange tree growing out of their living room floor...?

JOHNNY: I got it! I'll strip to my shorts. I'll put on a blindfold. I'll play the guitar....

NELLY: In the middle of the afternoon?

JOHNNY: ...you can sneak up on me, throw me on the floor, and put that delirious tongue of yours to work.

NELLY: But we have work to do, beautiful. Money to make.

JOHNNY: Give it a break, Nelly. How about this? You tie me to the hood of the red T-bird and lick me till I'm senseless.

NELLY: Hmmmmm, that sounds like fun....

JOHNNY: You know what's fun? Pour the orange juice on your skin. The feeling is incredible.

(NELLY *squeezes an orange on her hand.*)

NELLY: Wow. Hmmmmmmmmmmmmmmmm!

JOHNNY: You feel every little thing about three hundred percent more.

ACT ONE

NELLY: *(Smiles at him)* You're a wizard, Johnny, the way you make me feel.

(JOHNNY *cuts open another orange and rubs the juice on* NELLY's *neck and back. She closes her eyes, relishing it.)*

NELLY: Oh God. I feel like candy.

(She kisses him. Lights down on them.)

7

(Lights up on AUGIE, *who is now sitting in a wheelchair with square wheels. He looks terrible. His wife's laughter is coming from the offstage bedroom.* AUGIE *bangs on the door with an old broom.)*

AUGIE: CUT IT OUT! I'm not going to sit here and quietly decompose while you and your boyfriend sin against God and nature. *(Bangs on the door with the broom)* A woman your age! Mother of twenty-one children! Have some respect for the sacred vows we took, will ya?! *(Pounds on the door and the laughter subsides)* Think you're twenty-one years old again? Huh? Think you still have something to give a man? Huhn? What do you have? A couple of moldy orgasms? Just tell your boyfriend you went to school with his grandmother! We'll see his enthusiasm drop then, won't we? His enthusiasms will look pretty flaccid then, huh? *(Bangs on the wall)* GIVE ME BACK MY OLD WHEELCHAIR. I promise I won't try to escape again. *(Waits for an answer. The silence makes him panic.)* And why don't I hear my children and grandchildren walking around? Where are my babies? Why did they leave me? I wasn't so bad to them! All I hear are the groans of bears and the screams of wild monkeys. Has anybody fed those animals? I know they can smell me and they know I'm defenseless. Okay—tell my children I'll reinstate birthdays! Happy birthday to all them snotnoses! *(Bangs on the wall)* And I've learned my lesson! I had an epiphany! Biggest friggin' epiphany you ever saw! I'm a better man now! I'll never be the way I was! And, oh yeah, I think I want to EAT this week, okay?! And someone has to come here and kill the mold growing on my arms.

(A spotlight on NELLY *asleep on the couch.)*

AUGIE: And I want to know where what's-her-name is. My daughter. The only child in this zoo that treated me with due respect. She was here once. She opened windows for me. And sweet air swept into the room with busy fingers cleaning the filth from my skin...and hot sunlight cooked every last cold corner of this room and blasted the night to pieces...it was great! I saw little pieces of night, shrieking and squeaking and scrambling under all the furniture and hiding in all the cracks of the floor, because of her.

*(*AUGIE *dials the phone. It rings in* NELLY's *house. She wakes up. She looks at the phone. Shaking with fear, she just looks at it, not moving.* AUGIE *waits, then slams down the phone.)*

AUGIE: I can bring her back! All I have to do is remember her name. I know all their names. I can name all my kids. Oscar, Maritza, Nilda, Heriberto, Carlos, Marcos, Beto, Lizbeth, Jesus, Felicia, Che, Gloria, Antonio, Anita, Rosaline, Primitivo, Ping, Sylvia, Linda, and Freddie. *(Counts on his fingers)* That's twenty. Oscar, Maritza, Nilda, Heriberto, Carlos, Marcos, Beto, Lizbeth, Jesus, Felicia, Che, Gloria, Antonio, Anita, Rosaline, Primitivo, Ping, Sylvia, Linda, Freddie and, and, and...*who*? Goddammit, tell me, who is she?! Her smell stained the air in this room, making it blue and gray, like her two-color eyes! My precious girl... old what's-her-damn-friggin'-name...

ACT ONE 23

(He looks around sadly. NELLY *looks at the phone.*
JOHNNY *enters and stands behind her.)*

JOHNNY: I don't want him bothering you.

NELLY: Go to bed. I'll be fine.

*(*JOHNNY *remains, watching the action.* NELLY *looks at* AUGIE *and calls out softly.)*

NELLY: Hey! Dad!

*(*AUGIE *looks around for the source of the voice. Frightened, he bangs on the wall as* NELLY *watches.)*

AUGIE: Hey! I want to make babies with you! I know your body can still make babies. *(Grimacing)* That beautiful body I love so much. *(He waits. No response.)* Think I can't do it? Think I'm dead from the waist down? Well, it still works. It's still in good working order. *(Looks at his lap in amazement)* Yes it is. It's working again! Hurry up, take advantage of this, it's not going to last all night!

(With incredible effort, AUGIE *tries to push himself to his feet. It takes a long time.* NELLY *watches, spellbound.)*

NELLY: I put him in that chair. And Mom's not taking care of him.

JOHNNY: I want you to ravage me tonight. I want us to make beautiful babies tonight. I'll play the guitar like the wind for you.

*(*AUGIE *finally makes it to his feet.* NELLY *has an irresistible urge to help him.* AUGIE *lets go of the chair.* NELLY *gasps.)*

NELLY: I prayed to God he'd get hit. I prayed he'd never walk again.

*(*JOHNNY *grabs his guitar and tries to block* NELLY's *view of* AUGIE.*)*

JOHNNY: I was in the garage. I sang. Something happened to my voice. It was amplified all over the San

Fernando Valley and my voice bounced off the San Gabriel Mountains and young women heard it cruising down 101 and 405 and they drove red Fiats to my door.

(We see a projection of women listening to music.)

NELLY: *(Not listening)* My gray eye is killing me. *His* eye. I'm getting headaches and I can't sleep.

(AUGIE reaches for his zipper. But as he tries to unzip his pants, he loses his balance and falls. NELLY screams. JOHNNY pulls an orange from the tree.)

JOHNNY: Have an orange with me.

(NELLY ignores JOHNNY. She watches AUGIE lying helpless on the ground.)

(Offstage, his wife laughs as garbage begins to fall on the prostrate AUGIE. NELLY tries to keep from sobbing.)

8

(A spotlight on the garage. JOHNNY is happily playing guitar for an invisible crowd of admirers.)

JOHNNY: I know the business is hot now. You're going to open a new "Nelly and Johnny's" in Encino. But I've been thinking of other things. In a city that worships beauty like mine...where men without half my looks drive Porsches *that I have to fix*...I'm no longer content putting my eight-by-ten glossies in people's glove compartments. That will never make me a famous model.

(Spotlight on NELLY, in center room, looking at AUGIE)

NELLY: There are women driving into the garage every day. They come to look at you and they drive red Fiats. Isn't that enough?

JOHNNY: That's only a handful of women. Not even ten.

ACT ONE

NELLY: What do you want? *Millions* of women to want you?

JOHNNY: Well...yeah...why not? *(Laughs)* The other day, a woman in a red Fiat pulls in. She runs the biggest modeling agency in the southland. She has wild red hair and beautiful gorgeous white striking perfect little hands. She's in my fan club. *(Laughs again)* I happen to have my shirt off. She's staring at the thin sweaty finger of black hair that starts at my navel and points down, who-knows-where. She called me provocative. She gave me her card. In deference to you, I ripped it up. But then I taped it back together. But I ripped it up again. But I taped it back together. But I ripped it up again...

9

(NELLY *goes to* AUGIE. AUGIE *is under a pile of old food, pizza boxes, newspapers, candy wrappers, beer cans, dirty Pampers, etc. The smell in the room makes* NELLY *want to gag.*)

(JOHNNY *angrily turns to face* NELLY. *From underneath the garbage,* AUGIE *groans.*)

AUGIE: *(In pain)* OooooOooooOooooOooooOoooo...

JOHNNY: The three of us will kill each other.

NELLY: I can make it work.

AUGIE: OooooooooOooooOOoooooooooo...!

NELLY: I've eaten those oranges. I'm bigger and smarter. I see him for what he is—

JOHNNY: A hardened, indecent, cockroach-version of a man.

NELLY: Dying.

AUGIE: I said: oooooOoooooooooooooOooooo.

JOHNNY: His death will be a mercy for all of us.

NELLY: If I'm one person, I'm three. You, me, and—

JOHNNY: Bring him here and you'll be only two. You and—

NELLY: Don't threaten me, Johnny, I—

AUGIE: I repeat: oooOoooooooooooooooOooooo!

(NELLY *approaches the pile of garbage warily. She uncovers* AUGIE. *He is motionless. There's mold growing on his arms, mushrooms growing out of his chair.* NELLY *angrily opens the bedroom door.*)

NELLY: What the hell's wrong with you, Mom?! There's mold growing on your husband and all you can do is screw teenage boys!

(NELLY *slams the door and runs offstage.*)

JOHNNY: Okay. I'll go to this party tonight. Behind your back. I'll go with the woman in the red Fiat and the white hands who says I'm provocative. I'll play my guitar like old times.

(*A projection of* JOHNNY *wearing a tuxedo. It says: "Johnny Amengual, model." He looks at himself and smiles.*)

(NELLY *enters with a sponge and water. She cleans the mold from* AUGIE's *arms then carries him back to the wheelchair.*)

NELLY: The smell of animal shit in this house is nauseating. On the tenth floor you can hear the spider monkeys. They're big now. Eating Lizbeth's old toys. Playing with Sylvia's clothes. Wearing her shorts. Peeing on her bed. Warthogs are walking through Antonio's room. They're getting big ideas about turning you into lunch. (*Beat*) It's Nelly. Remember? Dad? No? Well, I'm taking you to Los Angeles. Eat this orange.

ACT ONE

(NELLY *gives* AUGIE *an orange. He eats viciously.*
AUGIE *visibly improves, as if electricity were shooting
through his body. He glares at* NELLY.)

NELLY: Hi.

AUGIE: Don't give me hi! There was a mold formation on my arms!

NELLY: Dad, I didn't have to come back—

AUGIE: —and do you know what your mother's doing in the next room? Huh, Pinhead?

NELLY: I am not a pinhead! And Mom was lonely! Your accident made her lonely.

AUGIE: That's heartbreaking! Of course, I wasn't lonely. I had the company of flies. The friendship of lice. She starves me! My children starve me. Why are my children doing this to me?

(NELLY *walks away from* AUGIE.)

NELLY: Because you were a piece of shit as a father, that's why.

AUGIE: What'd you say to me? I was a great father! I gave birth to twenty-one—

NELLY: Wrong, Dad. *Mom* gave birth. You gave *zip*. You weren't around. You were partying. *(Beat)*
We taught ourselves language, Dad. *There were no adults to teach us words.* That's why Primitivo, Nilda, and Heriberto can't *even speak*. Did you know that? No! You just thought they were shy! Lizbeth and Felicia speak in rhyme. Ping speaks in commercials. Gloria speaks nonsense. *Walking?!* Did you ever teach your kids walking? Anita hops like a rabbit. Rosaline walks on her hands. Social graces? Morals? Justice? *Hygiene?* No one taught us. Your poor children are compulsive liars and pyromaniacs and so love-starved, they'll sleep with the first person that smiles at them. *(Beat)* I grew

up in the middle of the storm, Dad, overlooked, uncounted, just one of twenty-one baby chicks, with my neck twisted up and my mouth open— waiting for you to bring down a single dead worm for all of us to eat and it wasn't enough, it was never enough, *and you want to know why everyone left?!*

(Beat)

AUGIE: Go back to California if you're going to be rude!

(NELLY *turns away from him in disgust.*)

NELLY: Oh, Dad...

(NELLY *faces* JOHNNY.)

AUGIE: And you know how your mother spent all the insurance money from the accident? Bought those four new Cadillacs sitting outside. And a new bed. A ten-thousand-dollar bed made out of *rose quartz*. And now she and her boyfriend are going on a vacation—that my shattered spine is paying for— to the Galapagos Islands!

(NELLY *wanders away from* AUGIE.)

NELLY: What did I come here to do, Johnny? Who is this old man and what do I want from him?

(JOHNNY *continues staring at the projection.*)

JOHNNY: I wish I could help you. But I'm looking at something so beautiful...

(NELLY *turns to* AUGIE, *determined. She's made up her mind and she's resolved to go all the way.*)

NELLY: C'mon, we're getting out of here.

AUGIE: Where? To a nursing home to rot—?

(NELLY *sweeps all the garbage offstage.*)

NELLY: We can afford you now. We have money.

ACT ONE   29

AUGIE: I will not live with Johnny Amengual.

NELLY: I've been working hard. Doing things no one ever taught me. Me and my *brains*.

AUGIE: I'll die in your house. I'll expire in two weeks, tops.

NELLY: But now I need a secretary. That's where you come in. It's light typing and phone. You don't need your legs for that.

AUGIE: A week and a half, max.

NELLY: A job will give you a purpose, keep your mind active, and it's not charity. It's the start of a new life, like it or not.

(NELLY *exits with* AUGIE.)

JOHNNY: *(To projection)* I have to find you Johnny Amengual, Model. Because she's doing it. She's bringing the butcher into my house.

(Lights out on JOHNNY. *The projection disappears.* NELLY *reenters, pushing* AUGIE *who is now sitting in a state-of-the-art wheelchair.)*

10

*(*JOHNNY *works on the car engine.* NELLY *wheels* AUGIE *into the garage. He and* JOHNNY *never look at each other.)*

NELLY: *(To* AUGIE*)* I just took out a loan to finance the opening of a third "Nelly and Johnny's," off the Long Beach Freeway, Firestone Exit, Southgate. Johnny and I have quadrupled our net worth since the start of the fiscal year. But we're very exclusive. In the Calendar we were listed as one of the ten hippest places in L A to get your car fixed. Sean Penn brings his '65 Oldsmobile for tune-ups. We've jump-started Marlon Brando and realigned Jack Nicholson. *(Goes to* JOHNNY *and laughs)* They love Johnny. He's a brilliant mechanic.

(NELLY *puts her arms around* JOHNNY *and kisses him. They intertwine rapidly.* AUGIE *watches, disgusted, as they walk offstage, kissing.* AUGIE *wheels himself out of the room. Lights change: it's night.)*

11

(AUGIE *is in the area L, lying on a hospital bed. His new room is a big improvement over the old one. There are plants, cozy pictures, etc. The rest of the house is completely black.)*

(From offstage, we hear NELLY *and* JOHNNY *making love.* AUGIE *listens, wide-eyed and revolted for a couple of moments. He covers his ears. He turns on his transistor radio. He hums. He tries anything he can to blot out the sound, but nothing works. He finally screams in frustration.)*

AUGIE: ARGHAAHAHHGRARGAHGAGGAH HAAAA!!

(Beat. NELLY, *quickly putting on a robe, enters.)*

NELLY: *(Breathless)* What happened? Something happened?

AUGIE: Yes! I had a terrible dream!

NELLY: You scared me to death. I thought the Walk-In Killer was getting you....

AUGIE: An indecent dream and you were in it.

NELLY: ...but you'll *live*, right? Go back to sleep...

AUGIE: Then I was seized by unbearable, wretching, cataclysmic pain in the soles of my feet.

NELLY: You have no feeling in your feet.

ACT ONE

AUGIE: My heart! Shooting, blistering, electric pain in the soles of my heart!

JOHNNY: *(Offstage)* Nelllyy! Come back!

NELLY: One second!

AUGIE: I can't deal with L A. Too many highways. Too much sun. Palm trees are weird. And there are rats living here!

NELLY: They live in the ivy *outside.*

AUGIE: They carry the plague. And they haven't caught the Hillside Strangler yet. And now there's this new one running around dressed up funny and cutting off your head politely. The Ninja Slasher.

NELLY: *(Yawns)* No. That's the Sepulveda Slasher. You're thinking of the Ninja Rapist.

JOHNNY: *(Offstage)* Nelly, *please*! Give me a break!

AUGIE: And I hate my job! My ear hurts because of that stupid telephone. Jack Nicholson was snotty to me. I'm going on strike.

NELLY: Go on strike, Dad, I'll cut your wages.

AUGIE: How can I pay the rent if you cut my wages?

NELLY: Exactly.

AUGIE: This is not how you treat a loving parent who gave you every advantage—

NELLY: That's true too.

AUGIE: I will not live with your revenge. I'd rather die than give you revenge!

NELLY: *(Tired)* I'm not trying to get revenge. I'm just...trying...to help you *make* something of yourself—

AUGIE: *(Softly)* I want my legs back. I want God to give me back my old life. The fun. The girls. I'm dead down there. If I can't sleep with a woman, what good am I? *(Quickly)* Find me a goat. If I kill a goat and wash my legs in its blood, I'll be walking in two weeks—

JOHNNY: *(Offstage)* Hey Nelllllllllllllllyyyyyyy! Come back to bed! I didn't finish yet! I have to finish!

NELLY: See you in the morning, Dad.

AUGIE: And please don't sleep with him anymore. I can't take it. He can finish his dirty business alone.

JOHNNY: *(Offstage)* NO I CAN'T! NELLLLLLLLLYYYYYYYY!

NELLY: *(To* AUGIE*)* Get some sleep. I'll see you later.

*(*NELLY *kisses* AUGIE *and quickly exits.)*

JOHNNY: *(Offstage)* Thank God you're back! Are you ready?

(We hear NELLY *and* JOHNNY *making love again.)*

(Beat)

AUGIE: Ahhhhhghghh! No! Nooooooo! Don't cut my throat! Don't kill me, please!

*(*NELLY *enters, putting on her robe. She gives* AUGIE *a murderous look.* AUGIE *smiles sheepishly. Lights start to fade.)*

(Before the lights disappear, NELLY *grabs her head as if getting a searing headache and we see a projection of* JOHNNY *wearing a white mask.)*

(Blackout)

END OF ACT ONE

ACT TWO

1

(A few months later. Lights up only on the orange tree. One by one, a third of the oranges in the tree turn black.)

2

(It's morning. NELLY, AUGIE *and* JOHNNY *are in the center room having breakfast.* JOHNNY *is in coveralls.* NELLY *is in a nice business suit.* AUGIE *is in* Star Wars *pajamas.)*

(No one eats. No one speaks. No one looks at the other person. Finally:)

NELLY: I heard on the radio: there's a hurricane coming from Japan. Be here today. Big mother hurricane the size of a hundred dragons. *(Laughs)* Maybe it'll drop Toshiba Microwaves on us! Huh? Nissan trucks and baby Godzillas falling from the sky! Paper birds. Sushi rain.

(No one laughs.)

NELLY: I made plans for this hurricane. You both have specific duties for this emergency plan of mine.

(No one says anything for a while.)

AUGIE: I have a complaint to make.

JOHNNY: Don't say a word. Not. A. Single. Friggin'. Word.

(Silence)

AUGIE: The hash browns? They suck.

JOHNNY: I said don't complain!

(Longer silence)

AUGIE: Hash browns should be crispy.

JOHNNY: Hash browns are any damn way I make 'em, pal. I am an excellent cook. I am multifaceted.

(Silence)

AUGIE: My room is too small. I want a bigger room. I want northern exposure.

(NELLY *quickly takes out a small notebook and reads from it.*)

NELLY: First, I'll shut down the garage. Disconnect the gas. Tape up windows. These are your duties, gentlemen. Dad, number one—

JOHNNY: *(To* NELLY*)* You ruined our paradise. Brought the friggin' serpent from Hell into our living room. So shut up.

AUGIE: Don't talk to my daughter that way.

JOHNNY: Your daughter? Your daughter? Your daughter? Your daughter? Your *daughter*? Don't tell me about your daughter—

AUGIE: I bet you can tell me all sorts of things about my daughters! Like which ones gave birth to your bastards before their sixteenth birthdays—

JOHNNY: *At least I loved them...*

AUGIE: How many of my babys' hearts did you break—?

JOHNNY: At least I know this one's name!

AUGIE: I do too! I do too! Her name is Carol!

JOHNNY: Her name is not Carol!

ACT TWO 35

AUGIE: Claudette?

(JOHNNY *grabs his guitar and starts to leave.*)

NELLY: Where are you going?

JOHNNY: There's always a party in Los Angeles. Look for me there.

AUGIE: Krista!

NELLY: We have to work on this. There's a hurricane—

AUGIE: Karen—

NELLY: *Nelly—*

AUGIE: I said my room sucks! I wouldn't keep a dog in that room. And why haven't you blessed me with legitimate grandchildren yet? What kind of man are you, anyway?

(JOHNNY *lunges at* AUGIE. *Loud hurricane winds. Thunder and lightning. We see a projection of a palm tree bent over by the wind.*)

JOHNNY: Goddamn everything.

(JOHNNY *goes to the garage. He closes windows, locks doors, etc.* NELLY *wheels* AUGIE *to his bed as the lightning quickens.*)

AUGIE: He's screwing other women. I can see it. I can tell.

NELLY: Keep your filthy mouth off him.

AUGIE: His walk is funny. He walks like a man screwing somebody who's not his wife.

(NELLY *angrily starts preparing* AUGIE's *bed.*)

JOHNNY: Gloria. Come rescue me! I'm in prison with your gelatinous old man and his gray gummy runny mucky fault-finding eyes.

(The wind picks up. There's a projection of Gloria. JOHNNY *sees the projection and kisses it as the wind howls.)*

NELLY: *(To* AUGIE*)* You? Bed.

*(*NELLY *starts to lift* AUGIE *into bed.* JOHNNY *kisses the projection of Gloria. He starts taking off his shirt. Lightning. Thunder. Gloria's projection turns off, along with all the lights onstage. It's a total blackout.)*

*(*JOHNNY *grabs flashlights and goes to* AUGIE *and* NELLY. *He gives* NELLY *and* AUGIE *a flashlight each.* AUGIE *is still in his chair, his radio playing. The storm gets louder, crazier.* JOHNNY *looks out the window.)*

JOHNNY: There are palm trees flying around! Cars going up in the air! All the stars on Hollywood Blvd. are whirling around like comets! The Hollywood Hills are cracking open and foul brown human cesspool goo is pouring out! If we only had a radio!

NELLY: Dad's got a radio.

JOHNNY: Augie's got a radio?

AUGIE: Don't get any ideas about this radio, junior. I'm listening to comedy.

JOHNNY: I want to hear the weather on the radio!

AUGIE: *(Listening to radio)* "The batter hits it to the shortstop. The shortstop throws it to the first baseman. Who gets it? Exactly."

JOHNNY: Listen to that wind! That's a wind we've never heard before. No one knows what's coming.

*(*JOHNNY *yanks the radio out of* AUGIE*'s hands. He throws the radio on the ground, smashing it.* AUGIE *looks at him in disbelief.)*

AUGIE: I'll kill you. No. I'll mutilate you first, then I'll kill you.

ACT TWO

(AUGIE *wheels himself to the bed. Lights up full all over the stage: power has returned. From under his pillow,* AUGIE *pulls out a massive machete. He goes after* JOHNNY *full speed.* JOHNNY *laughs.*)

AUGIE: Don't laugh at me!

(NELLY *lies on the hospital bed, playing with the buttons, making the bed go up and down.* JOHNNY *dances around* AUGIE, *taunting him.* AUGIE *nearly hits him several times.*)

JOHNNY: You're a joke! You're a vast human joke!

AUGIE: And you're going to be little, tiny, compact pieces of dead mechanic! Little, tiny, bloody, painful pieces of dead shit!

(*As* AUGIE *continues to swing the machete,* JOHNNY *plays his guitar, dancing around* AUGIE. AUGIE *stops, exhausted.* NELLY *continues playing with the bed.*)

AUGIE: My daughter isn't the only one with funny gray eyes. Look at mine. They're gray too. I can see the future too. You're going to die twice, Johnny Amengual. All men die once. But you're going to die twice.

(*As* JOHNNY *continues to dance and play the guitar, lights start to fade. In the dark, it's* JOHNNY's *wild laugh that echoes. Blackout.*)

3

(*Lights up on garage.* JOHNNY *is working on the car engine.* AUGIE, *in his chair stage left, is flipping over tarot cards.* NELLY *is on the sofa in the center room, vainly trying to concentrate on bookkeeping.*)

(*As* AUGIE *flips cards,* JOHNNY *holds his head as if going through an intense headache.*)

AUGIE: Johnny is vain. Johnny is ignorant. Johnny is perverted. Johnny is empty-headed. Johnny is lazy. Johnny is rude. Johnny is redundant. Johnny is derivative. Johnny is indecent. *(Smiles)* Gloria!

(JOHNNY hears "Gloria." He looks around, trying to figure out where the word came from.)

JOHNNY: Gloria.

(We see a projection of Gloria. JOHNNY can't help but look at her. AUGIE chants:)

AUGIE: Gloria is beautiful. Gloria is amoral. Gloria is self-actualized. Gloria is user-friendly. Gloria is upwardly mobile. Gloria is-tax exempt. Gloria is a virgin.

JOHNNY & AUGIRE: Gloria is a whore. Gloria is growth-oriented. Gloria is bicoastal. Gloria is generous. Gloria is waif-like. Gloria is legal.

AUGIE: Johnny! I'm legal!

(JOHNNY looks around. He rubs his throbbing head.)

JOHNNY: Gloria?

AUGIE: It's my birthday.

JOHNNY: Wait, wait a min—

AUGIE: I'm legal.

JOHNNY: ...this is crazy; where...are...you...?

AUGIE: It's my birthday.

JOHNNY: It's a headache.

AUGIE: I'm legal.

JOHNNY: ...aspirin, Johnny...you need to get some asp—

AUGIE: It's my birthday.

JOHNNY: Gloria? *Where? Are? You?*

ACT TWO   39

AUGIE: I'm legal.

JOHNNY: Really?

AUGIE: It's my birthday.

JOHNNY: I...I...don't believe....

AUGIE: I'm legal.

JOHNNY: I miss you. Is this real—?

AUGIE: It's my birthday.

JOHNNY: I know, baby! I know!

AUGIE: I'm legal.

JOHNNY: That's great. But.

AUGIE: It's my birthday.

JOHNNY: But. No. I love Nell—

AUGIE: I'm legal.

JOHNNY: I need...to get out of here...I need....

AUGIE: It's my birthday.

JOHNNY: ...to play the guitar...have a little fun...

AUGIE: I'm legal.

JOHNNY: ...Gloria?

AUGIE: Go.

JOHNNY: I need to go.

AUGIE: Go.

JOHNNY: Being a mechanic sucks...

AUGIE: *Go!*

(Gloria's projection disappears. JOHNNY *hurriedly takes off his coveralls—he's got party clothes underneath. He combs his hair, grabs his guitar. He and* NELLY *look at each other.)*

(During the following scene, AUGIE *looks at his tarot cards as if they were* NELLY *and* JOHNNY.*)*

JOHNNY: I can't anymore, Nelly, I can't!

AUGIE: It's my birthday!

JOHNNY: I don't know what's wrong—it could be an earthquake I feel vibrating in my bones like a bad omen—

NELLY: You're working too hard, John—

JOHNNY: I'm full of *static*...white noise behind my damn *eyes*....

NELLY: Come here. Sit with me.

JOHNNY: No! It's not fatigue. It's the day. It's Gloria's birthday, Nel. She's legal today.

AUGIE: I'm legal!

JOHNNY: She's been shoved into my mind, Nelly. She's telling me to break open the night and be wild in it.

AUGIE: It's my birthday!

JOHNNY: I looked at my greasy clothes today. The smell of transmission fluid and dirty valves. I'm permeated with this job, Nelly. It came to me today: I don't love my talent for cars.

AUGIE: I'm legal.

JOHNNY: I have to quit "Nelly and Johnny's." I'm ready to go. To start my true career as a model because I will never be better looking than I am now!

NELLY: Because it's Gloria's birthday?

JOHNNY: Because it's time. And we have security. A bank full of money. Forty-six skilled mechanics who can cover for me—.

NELLY: Because it's Gloria's birthday?

ACT TWO 41

JOHNNY: Because it's *me*. This is the man you married. I tried to do it your way...I worked hard...and I'm dead tired because my heart was never in it and I suffered too much.

(JOHNNY *goes to her. She holds him.* AUGIE *holds the tarot cards in the air.*)

AUGIE: Let him go let him go let him go let him go...

NELLY: *(To* JOHNNY*)* Go do what you want. Please go do what you want. Just—don't turn me into a jailer. I'm not your goddamn jailer.

(JOHNNY *looks at her, shocked—then jumps.*)

JOHNNY: All right! Oh this is it! Look out America! I'm going to be mobbed when I step out of the house in the morning! I'm going to be incredibly snotty to many people!

(NELLY *laughs. He looks at her.*)

JOHNNY: You don't mind? Do you mind? You mind, right?

NELLY: We were a great team, Johnny.

JOHNNY: Why don't you quit too? It can't be fun for you anymore. It's a machine. *Dump* it.

NELLY: But I love this machine.

JOHNNY: Then just go out with me tonight. Put on your best dress. Every jewel you own. Something sparkly and diamond-like that'll shiver when you dance.

NELLY: I can't.

JOHNNY: Come on! One little night! This is a party town! We'll dress up like barbarians and drive Martin Sheen's Porsche.

NELLY: I just can't. I'm too afraid.

JOHNNY: Of having a little fun?

NELLY: Of turning my back on the work I have to do.

JOHNNY: For one night?

NELLY: I don't want everything to disappear when I'm not looking. Things have been disappearing from my life for as long as I remember.

JOHNNY: That was your old life.

NELLY: Clothes, people, food—*food already in my stomach* has been taken away from me. If I stop working...if I let down for just one night...I'll start speaking in nonsense... walking around on all fours....

JOHNNY: I know what's happening. It's. It's *him*. Augie.

AUGIE: Don't blame me! Hey!

JOHNNY: He's doing something to you too. He's bringing that old life back to you.

NELLY: You can't blame him for everything. I laid down the law with him. He's quiet. Hardly leaves his room now.

JOHNNY: He's doing something. Putting things in the food.

NELLY: He stopped doing that a long time ago—

JOHNNY: *(Desperate) Something's* changed with me. I don't dream in color anymore. When I *think*...I can't hear my voice too well...I miss the sound of my *thoughts,* Nelly...he's taken that away.

AUGIE: I can't do that! I never learned to do that!

NELLY: Johnny, all he's doing is his goat ritual. He wants to kill a goat, wash his legs in its blood, and walk again.

JOHNNY: Let him. Let him walk three thousand miles out of our lives.

NELLY: No sacrificial killing in my house!

ACT TWO

JOHNNY: But all the oranges are turning *black* because of him! He's back in your blood. He controls your sleep. He controls your dreams. He's *corrupting* you. And did you notice? Now our house is getting bigger! There are rooms up there starting to grow!

NELLY: That's crazy—

JOHNNY: Well, he's not going to corrupt me! I'm going out to find some fun! I'm going to find my fan club! To find the lady in the red Fiat! *(Grabs his guitar and starts to exit. He looks at* NELLY.*)* I miss the old times, Nelly. When guys would bristle when I walked into a room and all their women looked at me. When I made time stop. People would whisper about me. Hearts would beat fast. Men would reach for their guns. Who would I talk to? Who would I dance with? Who would I touch? I have to prove I have the old magic.

(JOHNNY *leaves.* AUGIE *clasps his hands in prayer and looks up at the sky.*)

NELLY: Be careful. You'll get yourself killed, Johnny.

4

(*Exhausted,* NELLY *lies on the sofa in the center room. Her eyes hurt. As* AUGIE *wheels himself around and around her, time passes rapidly. Black and white clouds pass overhead.* NELLY *tries to sleep and can't.*)

AUGIE: He was right. I am part of you again. I'm your angel. I'm back in your blood.

NELLY: What are you doing to him? I keep hearing the flap-flap-flap of tarot cards in your room.

AUGIE: He knows it's Gloria's birthday because *those two are linked*. They're going to be together no matter what you do, Carmen.

NELLY: My name's not Carmen!

AUGIE: You have to run. Tonight. Run with me to the old house and live like old times.

NELLY: I will never go back there.

AUGIE: You're smart and strong and beautiful. There's no reason to live your life for him *when you can live your life for me*. I'll always appreciate you, Cathy.

NELLY: *(Tired)* That's not my name!

AUGIE: Doesn't matter what your name is. You're *my* girl. Augie's girl. The one I knew would come back and clean the sticky mold off my body—

NELLY: I'm tired, Dad. I'm really tired. And I don't trust you.

AUGIE: You married him to get out of my house. But there's no escaping my house. It's always with you. Always growing in you, room after unbelievable room, containing strange and magical things.

NELLY: *(More to herself)* My eyes hurt. If I don't go to sleep now, I'll be awake the rest of the month....

AUGIE: Don't fight me.

NELLY: ...and I don't want to start seeing the future. I don't want to start seeing things I don't want to see!

AUGIE: You think you can remake the world. Turn Johnny into an honest man. Make us all live together. Well you can't. You're not that strong.

NELLY: And you. No *more*—please—find yourself a friggin' goat—kill it—walk again—and get the hell out of my house! You're fired! I'm getting someone else to work for me. I'm sending you back to Mom.

AUGIE: You're confused.

NELLY: Don't tell me that!

ACT TWO   45

(She slaps AUGIE.*)*

*(*JOHNNY *staggers into the center room, guitar shattered, clothes torn, and face bloody. He stands in a special light.* AUGIE *wheels himself to his bedroom.* NELLY *looks at her husband in shock.)*

JOHNNY: It was six of them against me...six jealous husbands...at least seven feet tall....

NELLY: I'll kill them. Whoever touched you, I'll get them, Johnny

JOHNNY: ...I fought back...I hit them hard...but their bodies were made of rock and they broke my hands....

NELLY: What did they look like? Where did they go?

JOHNNY: ...the husbands were pissed...didn't like my fan club...six animals in black tie and brass knuckles and steel-pointed boots and not a teardrop's worth of mercy....

*(*NELLY *cleans* JOHNNY's *bloody face.* AUGIE *stifles a laugh and starts flipping over tarot cards.* NELLY *takes* JOHNNY *to the sofa and he lies down.)*

5

(Lights change. NELLY *is on the phone,* JOHNNY *is on the sofa,* AUGIE *is in his area stage left.)*

NELLY: I want police protection. For my husband. He's been getting death threats. Jealous husbands have burned him in effigy on La Cienega Blvd. Armies of angry men come here daily to shake dangerous weapons in his face. I want a cop in front of the garage twenty-four hours a day. And a police escort to follow Johnny to all the modeling agencies in town. As soon as his face clears, he's going to have a big career as a model. Yes, Johnny is too beautiful to live! Yes, it's the kind of beauty other men want to kill him for. Do I have to get a gun? I have chic friends with guns. I'll protect him myself!

(NELLY *hangs up.* AUGIE *goes to* JOHNNY, *whispers.*)

AUGIE: You're going back out.

(JOHNNY *sits up, dazed, rubbing his head.*)

JOHNNY: I'm going back out.

NELLY: You're not going anywhere.

JOHNNY: There's a party somewhere in Los Angeles.

NELLY: You're delirious.

JOHNNY: I'm going back out.

AUGIE: Let him go out! A man shouldn't be afraid to leave his house.

JOHNNY: I'm not afraid. I'm going out. There's a party somewhere in Los Angeles!

NELLY: You're not going anywhere.

AUGIE: *(To* JOHNNY*)* Are you afraid? Or are you a man?

JOHNNY: I'm a man! I'm a man! I'm a man!

(JOHNNY *starts to wobble to the door.* NELLY *exits and reenters with a revolver. She points it at* JOHNNY.)

NELLY: I happen to be real serious about this. I want obedience in this matter! I know about danger. I was raised on it. It was in the milk. It sets off a vibration in your gut, in the frightened liquids of your intestines: my dreams are thick with it. I'm closing the garage. Sealing us off from the rest of the world until I figure out what to do about this danger.

(JOHNNY *lies on the sofa.*)

(NELLY *goes to the garage. As she enters, she sees something on the ground and screams,* JOHNNY *sits up startled, and a*

ACT TWO

projection of a human hand is shown. Lights favor JOHNNY. *Others freeze.)*

JOHNNY: *(Stunned)* Did he have to do that to her? Did he have to chop off her hand? It was innocent! She wanted to know where I got my hair cut. What diet I was on. What gym I worked out at.

(NELLY *rushes to* JOHNNY, *shaking, frightened.)*

JOHNNY: Now her jealous husband's chopped off the beautiful hand that never touched me but wanted to...

NELLY: Oh Johnny. My eyes have been totaled by that amputated hand on the garage floor—oh—God—how that poor woman must have suffered...

JOHNNY: My face. My beautiful face. I did that to her.

(NELLY *is fighting her body's tendency to drop down on all fours.)*

NELLY: No. No. *Upright* Nelly. Be upright. Don't sink back, that's what your enemies want.

JOHNNY: How many more will suffer for me?

(The projection of the severed hand disappears.)

NELLY: This wasn't just an act of cruelty. It signals war. They're coming for you. *(Exits and reenters with a bullet proof vest)* They're capable of anything. Even if we lock the doors and smother ourselves behind barred windows, they'll find a way in. Armed Response won't stop them. *(Puts on the vest)* I know where they live. I have lists. I know all the red Fiats we repaired. I know where they get together to plot severed hands and mayhem.

(She sticks the revolver into her belt. She goes to AUGIE. *She searches his room for the machete.)*

AUGIE: You won't find them.

NELLY: I have lists! Computer lists. Shut up. You think I'm weak? You think I'm still that four-legged little mouse you used to bat around? I'm about to fulfill my potential.

AUGIE: Ain't feminine.

NELLY: Is too! Where's the fucking machete? *(Finds the machete)* Ah-ha! You're going to stand guard. Okay? Just do it. I won't be home. I have a mission.

AUGIE: All your energy wasted being tough.

NELLY: It's how I survived your house, Dad. Now. I don't want you to let anyone in. If they come near my husband, I want you to slash them thoroughly. *(Hands him the machete)* If I come home and he's dead...I will take this machete and amputate your lifeless dick.

(NELLY kisses AUGIE on the cheek, goes to JOHNNY and kisses him.)

NELLY: And you. Step out of the house, I'll kill you. Bye, honey. *(She exits.)*

(With the machete on his lap, AUGIE wheels himself to JOHNNY in the center room. He watches JOHNNY sleep. He lifts the machete in the air as if about to chop JOHNNY's head off.)

AUGIE: Hey! Are you my goat?! Are you the sacrifice I need?

JOHNNY: *(Asleep)* Gotta get new pictures.

AUGIE: You're as good as a goat. Stupid like a goat. I could cut your friggin' head right off. Smear your blood all over my legs, wash them real good, and run away and be happy the rest of my life.

JOHNNY: *(Asleep)* Get some new clothes. Drop ten pounds. Now that Nelly's behind me, I'm going all the way.

ACT TWO

(AUGIE *lifts the machete as if to cut off* JOHNNY's *head. He brings down the machete swiftly—but stops himself at the last second. He brings the sharp edge of the machete gently down on* JOHNNY's *neck and laughs.*)

AUGIE: There are better ways, Augie. Less blood.

(*The projection of Gloria is seen.*)

AUGIE: Johnny!

JOHNNY: Gloria!

AUGIE: It's me, baby. Tell me. Are all those messy death threats and severed hands getting you down?

JOHNNY: I'm scared.

AUGIE: Don't be blue, Johnny. There's good news. I'm in town. I'm here in Los Angeles.

JOHNNY: You are?

AUGIE: And guess what! I have two-color eyes. I talk to my big sisters. Lizbeth, Maritza, and Felicia tell me how wonderful you are.

JOHNNY: Come over here!

AUGIE: I can't. Your wife what's-her-name is there. Come to me. I'm at the Toluca Lake Capri Motel.

JOHNNY: I can't leave. Nelly'd kill me.

AUGIE: Once we're together, I can give you the life you want.

JOHNNY: Jealous men will firebomb me if they see me in my car.

(*The projection of a car is seen.*)

AUGIE: I know you can't be satisfied by one woman. You need new women with new eyes. Soon, my little sister Anita will be legal in many states. When that day comes, I'll cheerfully let you go....

JOHNNY: You will? *(Quickly)* But they'll burn me.

AUGIE: I'm here one night. This is our last chance.

JOHNNY: ...I want to....

AUGIE: So get in your car, pick two fat oranges from your magic tree and meet me at the Toluca Lake Capri Motel.

(JOHNNY *goes to the orange tree and picks two huge oranges.*)

JOHNNY: Nelly...?

AUGIE: My father will cover for you. He'll swear you were here all night.

(JOHNNY *looks around.*)

JOHNNY: Nell? I'm sorry. She's in my blood. I'm a weak man. I'm not good like you.

(JOHNNY *exits. Hold on projection of the car.* AUGIE *pops a wheelie and holds up the machete, victorious.*)

6

(*As* AUGIE *laughs,* NELLY *enters the center room, her gun smoking. She seems intoxicated.*)

NELLY: Johnny! Johnny! Haha! I was your Clint Eastwood, Johnny! And they made my day!

AUGIE: He's not here. He's out fooling around. Cheating on you.

NELLY: *(Laughing)* I didn't kill. But I maimed. I left behind a few legs with holes in them, a few splintered bones, and some shot-up hands. I blasted their cars to rusty pulp!

AUGIE: Doing it with your baby sister in a cheap Toluca Lake motel. I begged him not to go out.

ACT TWO   51

NELLY: We live in a safe world. I cleaned it out for you. It's now safe for people who love each other like you and me.

(A huge explosion. The projection of the car is replaced by a projection of a car in flames.)

(JOHNNY staggers in, clothes smoking. He covers his face with his hands. NELLY attends to him as if putting out a fire on his body. The projection of the flaming car disappears. Lights down low until there's only light around NELLY and JOHNNY.)

7

(Tableau: NELLY *holding* JOHNNY. JOHNNY *facing upstage.* NELLY *facing downstage.* AUGIE *in darkness.)*

JOHNNY: Nelly, they rigged the car.

NELLY: You'll be out of the hospital in one month. *(Beat)* We lost the garage. It went up in flames. People are avoiding "Nelly and Johnny's." The Calendar's listed us as one of the top ten places to avoid in Los Angeles. *(Beat)* Your body wasn't touched by the fire—but you didn't escape the flames altogether.

JOHNNY: When can I go home? I feel fine. I don't have a single burn.

NELLY: Remember that it doesn't matter. Nothing's changed. You're still the same man. I still love you.

*(*NELLY *holds up a white mask.)*

JOHNNY: Why did they cover all the mirrors in my room?

NELLY: The jealous men have stolen your precious beauty from this unlucky world. It's your first death—my father predicted it.

JOHNNY: I'm all right! I'm fine! I wasn't touched!

NELLY: So this is your new face.

JOHNNY: Why do they keep me here? *(He turns to face the audience.)*

NELLY: Look up. Up.

JOHNNY: Why did they cover all the mirrors in my room?

(JOHNNY *looks up.* NELLY *brings the mask down on his face. When it touches him, he screams.* NELLY *straps the skintight mask to his face and holds him.)*

8

(NELLY *takes* JOHNNY *to the sofa.* AUGIE *is joyfully flipping over tarot cards, barely able to contain his glee.* AUGIE *wears a Walkman.)*

NELLY: Dinner—will be—will be—ready—*okay, I will not start talking funny! (Slow)* I can't—be—slipping—back. You see what happens Johnny? Everything goes! I will straighten up my speech! Grief will not destroy my language! *(Determined)* Dinner will be ready in a couple of minutes! *(Beat, normal)* Dinner will be ready in a couple of minutes. *(Beat)* It hurts to walk upright. Your accident's made my back curve down. Ever since your fire. Ever since your meltdown. But I'm holding myself up. For you and Dad and what's left of the business—I'm engaged in a struggle to *make life work again.* There will be fresh asparagus for dinner. Mashed potatoes, roast beef and fresh milk. Okay?

(NELLY *waits. No response from* JOHNNY.)

AUGIE: He always traded on his good looks to get away with murder. What's he going to do without his secret weapon?

ACT TWO 53

NELLY: He's going to survive on my strength.

AUGIE: Yours? Are you stupid? Did you see the get-well cards from all the women he used to sing for?

NELLY: I beat my past. I slaughtered my inheritance. I maimed my bad speech and my crooked legs. I will beat this catastrophe too, Dad.

AUGIE: You know he keeps that woman's severed hand in a baggie? Look in your closet. It's there. Next to the shoes. He can look at it every day and remember the power of his lost beauty.

NELLY: Get up and let's have dinner, Johnny.

(She waits. He's motionless.)

NELLY: No? You're not hungry? *(Beat. Soft)* Maybe you'll eat an orange with me? Oranges always make you want to play guitar.

(NELLY *kisses* JOHNNY *and takes his hand.*)

NELLY: The modeling agencies have been calling nonstop. They loved your old pictures. They can find you work instantly. Uhm. I told them you weren't available. They offered big contracts and I had to say no. I burned all your old pictures, Johnny, I had to. *(Beat)* I don't care about it. Means nothing to me. Your face was not what I loved when I loved.

(NELLY, *trying not to cry, exits. Lights fall. It's night.*)

9

(JOHNNY *on the sofa.* AUGIE *in the center room.* NELLY *enters center room with a box of masks.)*

NELLY: Look at me. I understand it's hard, Johnny. I'm suffering too. But I have to *do* something. I have to keep moving. *(Beat)* I reopened "Nelly and Johnny's." I'm working again. Twenty-four hours a day. Got on the phone to old customers. Begged them to come back. Told them it's safe. They're coming back!

(No response. NELLY looks at him a while.)

NELLY: Try these other masks. Maybe you'll feel better.

(NELLY takes a mask out of the box. It's a Cary Grant mask. She puts it over JOHNNY's white mask. She doesn't like the way it looks. She tries another mask—a Donald Duck mask. That doesn't look right either and she tries another.)

NELLY: *(To AUGIE:)* I told his little groupies to go to hell. I threatened to blow them away.

AUGIE: Don't you ever give up? That's not a man. That's a tackling dummy.

NELLY: Did you see the *L A Times*? The jealous husbands have taken out a full-page ad congratulating themselves for doing this to Johnny. I should have killed them all.

AUGIE: Me? I'm a real man with real needs, but you ignore me for *that*.

NELLY: I'm going to make Johnny come back. I'm going to improve his self-image. Get him going again.

AUGIE: Listen. You have to do the only honorable thing. The only moral thing. A mercy killing.

NELLY: *(Looks at him)* What did you say?

AUGIE: He's worthless. At least I can answer the phone and type.

NELLY: He still has his hands! He can still function!

(NELLY pulls JOHNNY to the car engine. AUGIE follows.)

AUGIE: Just kill him! Kill him and remarry! Live in the old house with me! Fill the old house with twenty-one children!

ACT TWO

(NELLY *makes* JOHNNY *stand in front of the engine.*)

NELLY: His hands have memories of usefulness and hard work. That's not dead in him.

AUGIE: You've got guns. It would be so easy to off him. And then you could blame it on a jealous husband—.

NELLY: Johnny. This is Chevy engine. It needs a tune-up. Show me you can still do it. Show me you can still make it go.

(JOHNNY *does not move.*)

NELLY: C'mon. Your hands are not burned. Your mind is not burned. Work is good for you. Work is important. Work keeps the spirit alive. Come on, Johnny.

(JOHNNY *doesn't move.* NELLY *grabs his hands angrily.*)

NELLY: Are you in prison, Johnny? Well, I'm in prison too! Goddamn you! *(She lets his hands go and walks away.)* I put my hands on your face. After the fire. I was holding in the guts of your face. But you're lost. And now it looks like I'm lost too. *My* face is burned. My eyes are burned *white....* *(Fighting for control)* ...white, my love, like the screaming brains trying to squeeze out of your eyes—blind old brains enraged with heat, trying to escape that hot oven and the simmering nerves and the baked memories and the bubbling dreams—just trying to run out of that head and into the cool air...

(NELLY *turns away, not wanting to let* JOHNNY *see her cry.* AUGIE *looks at* NELLY *and smiles.*)

AUGIE: Mercy. Killing. Today.

(NELLY *moves to slap him across the face. He grabs her hand and stops her.*)

AUGIE: Tonight, if you can sleep, dream the future, dream next year, and you'll see it doesn't contain him.

NELLY: I'm throwing you out!

AUGIE: I'm your father. I know what's best. I even know your name begins with an "N." I know more than he does!

NELLY: You're going back to Mom. GOING BACK TODAY!

AUGIE: That vegetable doesn't know anything. Ask him. Ask him your name!

NELLY: I don't have to test him.

AUGIE: What's your wife's name, Johnny?

NELLY: Leave him alone.

AUGIE: What is her name? Tell me her name!

NELLY: *(To* JOHNNY*)* Don't have to tell him anything!

(Beat)

JOHNNY: I don't know.

(Beat)

NELLY: What, Johnny?

AUGIE: He doesn't know.

(Beat)

JOHNNY: I don't remember.

NELLY: *(Shocked)* It's Nelly. My—my—my—name—.

JOHNNY: I don't know it. I'm sorry.

NELLY: Say name! My name! *(Panicking)* What's my goddamn name?

(Beat)

JOHNNY: Pinhead...?

*(*AUGIE *laughs.)*

NELLY: What?

ACT TWO 57

AUGIE: *(Laughing)* Pinhead!

NELLY: Johnny?

AUGIE: He called you Pinhead!

(AUGIE *laughs.* NELLY *leaves the stage.* AUGIE *sees his chance and hurries to* JOHNNY.)

AUGIE: You smashed my radio. But I adapted. Now I have a Walkman. I'm a survivor. I don't think you're a survivor. You still smell like the fire. I lost my appetite for a week because of the barbecue smell of your skin. Wanna listen to my radio now?

(*He puts the Walkman on* JOHNNY. *We hear horrible, dissonant sounds: human cries, wind, electric noise.*)

AUGIE: Listen to the hurricane now. To the world out of control all around you. The chaos of deferred dreams. The riot of sexual rejection. You think Gloria wants to nuzzle up against that charred stump of yours? Or Anita? Or Rosaline?

(AUGIE *takes the Walkman off* JOHNNY. *The sounds disappear.*)

AUGIE: Your wife won't do you the favor of a mercy killing. So you have to take the initiative. A nice, clean suicide is the best way. *(He wheels himself to the orange tree.)* See this? Some oranges have turned black. They're sour inside. They're no longer the sweet aphrodisiac you seduced my dear daughter what's-her-name with. The grief in this house has turned the juice in each orange into high-octane gasoline. Really flammable. Smell.

(AUGIE *plucks a black orange from the tree and puts it under* JOHNNY's *nose.* JOHNNY *sniffs and quickly jerks away.*)

AUGIE: Pure gasoline. Very explosive. The key to your freedom.

(NELLY *enters with a suitcase. She goes to* AUGIE.)

NELLY: I want you to get the hell out of my house!

AUGIE: Why? What'd I do...?

NELLY: Get out, you parasitic, caustic, irrational, lethal, inconsiderate, possessive, demeaning, disgusting, degenerate old man!

AUGIE: Your name begins with an N! It's Naomi!

NELLY: *He* is the man I love! *He* went through hell for me. *He* gave up his dreams for me. I will not abandon such a man!

AUGIE: Norma? Nina?

NELLY: How could I have been so stupid? How could I not have seen you sooner? Seen you for what you really—really—really—really—. *(She falls to the ground. She starts running around on all fours.)*

AUGIE: That's my girl! That's the girl I love! I'll take care of you now!

NELLY: No—!

AUGIE: Run, run, little girl! You're so cute when you scamper!

NELLY: I can fight this—!

AUGIE: Your name! *It's coming back to me....*

NELLY: ...*I can stop this....*

AUGIE: Ne—Ne—Ne—*Nel*—.

NELLY: I'm fighting. I'm fighting. I'm fighting. *(She stops running.)* I'm fighting you. *(She straightens up with great difficulty.)*

AUGIE: *(Panicking)* Ne—Ne—Nel—Ne—Ne—.

NELLY: Nelly, Nelly, it's Nelly—. *(She dashes to* AUGIE's *suitcase.)*

ACT TWO 59

NELLY: *(Out of breath)* You're going back home to Mom. Your bags are packed. You leave in one hour.

AUGIE: Let me prove I love you!

NELLY: I called home. Mom and her boyfriend are getting married and moving to the Galapagos Islands. You have the house all to yourself—.

AUGIE: Johnny! Tell her I can't go back! I'll die in that house!

NELLY: I'll hire a nurse to walk you and cook for you.

AUGIE: Alone? With all the memories in that house?

NELLY: When Johnny's back on his feet, I'll visit you. Christmas maybe.

AUGIE: The animals! My grandchildren's hungry animals! They'll eat me alive!

NELLY: I hope so.

AUGIE: You're sending me to my death! I won't go!

(NELLY *pulls out the revolver and points it at* AUGIE.)

NELLY: You'll go. And you'll like it.

(NELLY *picks up the suitcases and leaves the house. As* AUGIE *wheels himself out, he stops near* JOHNNY.)

AUGIE: Remember to cleanse yourself, Johnny. In oranges. *(He wheels himself out.)*

10

(*Lights up in* AUGIE's *old bedroom L.* NELLY *enters, pushing* AUGIE, *who is sitting in the square-wheeled chair.*)

NELLY: I can't believe how big the house has gotten. Almost covers the block.

AUGIE: I'll die of loneliness.

NELLY: You gave birth to twenty-one children, how can you be lonely?

AUGIE: I miss Los Angeles! The palm trees. The sun. The big lovely room I lived in. The Midnight Stalker! The plague!

(NELLY *can barely look at him.*)

NELLY: I don't know what to say to you, Dad. I thought there was something else in you. Something...what?... good? Does that word remotely apply to you? What was good, Dad? That you loved me enough to wish Johnny dead? Should that make me happy? *(Beat)* My grey eye. Gives me sight. That's from you. Sight is good. But when I think of some of the things you've said and done...I almost want to scrape my grey eye out with a stick, Dad, and go blind.... *(She kisses him quickly. She starts to exit.)*

AUGIE: Your name is Nelly.

(She stops. AUGIE *can barely look at her.)*

AUGIE: Nelly was your mother's mother's name. She was a brave old lady with different color eyes who could see the future in her sleep. Old Nelly averted disasters by dreaming them before they happened. Hurricanes, droughts, insect invasions. But her talent took its toll. Every time she predicted a disaster she absorbed the fear for all her people and that made her grey, feeble, fragile, before her time. She drank heavily to calm her electrified nerves. She died young. A hero. Nelly is my eleventh child, my fifth daughter. Oscar, Maritza, Nilda, Heriberto, Carlos, Marcos, Beto, Lizbeth, Jesus, Felicia, Che, Gloria, Antonio, Anita, Rosaline, Primitivo, Ping, Sylvia, Linda, Freddie and the one who stuck by me the longest, the one we called Nelly.

ACT TWO

(NELLY *looks at her father. Lights up on the center room.* JOHNNY *sits motionless on the sofa, waiting.*)

NELLY: Christmas. Maybe.

(NELLY *exits.* AUGIE *is alone. Light starts coming down on him.*)

AUGIE: Get back here. Hey Pinhead! Pinhead! I made that up! It wasn't real! But it almost worked, huh? I almost had you going, didn't I, Pinhead?

(AUGIE *looks around, truly frightened. The door to the offstage bedroom opens and he stares into the room— what he sees in there shocks him.*)

AUGIE: Oh my God.

(*We hear the low growl of a large carnivore. It's joined by other animal sounds—growls, shrieks, the flap of wings— getting louder, sounding strange and unnatural.* AUGIE *covers his ears, knowing this is the end.*)

AUGIE: C'mon Augie. What do you have to say now? Nothing? No apology? No remorse? No prayer? No farewell speech? No cursing? No lamentation? *(Beat)* No confession?

(AUGIE *screams. Animal noises stop.*)

11

(NELLY *enters the center room. The other rooms are dark.* NELLY *sits on the sofa with* JOHNNY.)

NELLY: So what do you say? Let's eat a few oranges and make wild, beautiful babies. It's been a long time, Johnny. We need to make ourselves feel good again and forget our worries. Do you want to?

JOHNNY: No.

NELLY: Are you sure?

JOHNNY: Yes.

NELLY: Never?

JOHNNY: How?

NELLY: Easy! The old fashioned way. I take off your clothes, you take off mine, we get on top of each other—you remember.

JOHNNY: I'm too ugly.

NELLY: No!

JOHNNY: I'll make ugly babies.

NELLY: You won't make ugly babies—.

JOHNNY: I'll make ugly babies! I will! I'll make ugly babies covered in scar tissue with their lips burned off and third-degree burns on their baby-blue eyes! Forget it. *(Beat)* Please forget it.

(Beat)

NELLY: Never?

(JOHNNY *doesn't answer.*)

NELLY: I'll make you change your mind. I'm not giving up. It's going to take some work, but we will have our old life back. *(She stands.)* I have to go to Encino. The "Nelly and Johnny's" there is in deep trouble. They need me. I won't be long.

JOHNNY: *(Sadly)* I'm sorry about everything. Goodbye.

NELLY: *(Not sure what he means)* Goodbye? Goodbye to you.

(NELLY *exits.* JOHNNY *alone*)

ACT TWO

12

(A red sunset washes the stage. JOHNNY *is motionless for a moment. Then he stands.)*

JOHNNY: Johnny is vain. Johnny is ignorant. Johnny is perverted. Johnny is empty-headed. Johnny is self-centered. Johnny is sleazy. Johnny is redundant. Johnny is derivative. *(He plucks a black orange from the tree, cuts it open and pours the cold gasoline from the orange over the furniture.)*

(Then he douses himself in the gasoline. He reaches into his pocket for a lighter, flicks on the flame and the stage is brilliant, bright red.)

*(*JOHNNY *takes off the mask as imaginary flames engulf him. We see a projection of a burning house. As he burns:)*

JOHNNY: Nelly is good. Nelly is clever. Nelly is fierce. Nelly is loyal. Nelly is warm. Nelly is kind. Nelly is…Nelly is…is…is…is. Nelly is.

(All the areas of the stage are wrapped in flames. The light hits a bright peak and then slowly fades to black.)

13

(Somewhere in front of the house, NELLY *runs on, on all fours—a spotlight following her for a moment. Then she starts running around and around, as the spotlight gets smaller and smaller.)*

(Just before it disappears, NELLY *shoots to her feet as if every muscle in her body were electrified. She stands. Blackout)*

END OF PLAY

www.ingramcontent.com/pod-product-compliance
Lightning Source LLC
Chambersburg PA
CBHW060218050426
42446CB00013B/3101